REPORT ON THE STATE OF UK-BASED RESEARCH ON LATIN AMERICA AND THE CARIBBEAN

2014

Edited by
Antoni Kapcia and Linda A Newson

INSTITUTE OF
LATIN AMERICAN
STUDIES

SCHOOL OF ADVANCED STUDY
UNIVERSITY OF LONDON

British Library Cataloguing-in-Publication Data
A catalogue record for this book is available from the British Library

ISBN 978-1-908857-12-5

INSTITUTE OF
LATIN AMERICAN
STUDIES

SCHOOL OF ADVANCED STUDY
UNIVERSITY OF LONDON

Institute of Latin American Studies
School of Advanced Study
University of London
Senate House
London WC1E 7HU

Telephone: 020 7862 8844
Fax: 020 7862 8886

Email: ilas@sas.ac.uk
Web: http://ilas.sas.ac.uk

Contents

Acknowledgements

This report had its genesis in the British Academy's Latin America and Caribbean Area Panel. The project was overseen by a steering group chaired by Professor Antoni Kapcia (University of Nottingham), and comprising Professor James Dunkerley (Queen Mary University of London), Dr David Howard (University of Oxford), Dr Peter Lambert (University of Bath), Professor Nicola Miller (University College London), Professor Maxine Molyneux (UCL Institute of the Americas), and Professor Linda Newson (King's College London and Institute of Latin American Studies).

Research was undertaken, in 2009–10, by Dr Diana Pritchard, currently Research Associate in Global Studies, University of Sussex. It was supplemented, in 2012–13, by Dr Sally Evans, Honorary Research Fellow in the University of Liverpool's School of Languages, Cultures and Area Studies. During the research more than one hundred people from universities, government departments, funding agencies, cultural institutions and non-governmental organisations (NGOs), were interviewed or contributed information. Thanks are due to everyone who committed their knowledge, views and time to the production of this report. While it would not have been possible without the generous financial support provided by the British Academy, the views expressed here do not necessarily represent those of the Academy.

The importance of carrying out research on Latin America and the Caribbean

The Latin American and Caribbean (LAC) region comprises a population of some 600 million, has the greatest income inequality in the world and the largest energy reserves outside the Middle East, and (more worryingly) is the region which produces an estimated 65–70 per cent of the cocaine on British streets. It has unquestionably weathered the post-2008 financial crisis and subsequent global recession better than some other parts of the world. The overall picture is one of an economically flourishing region, led by economies such as Brazil, Mexico, Colombia and Chile, contrasting starkly with the image of Latin America during the so-called 'lost decade' of the 1980s, the years of hyperinflation, massive indebtedness and deep recession.

Over the last two decades, more democratic systems of governance appear to have been successfully consolidated across the region. As a result, Latin American countries are now playing an increasingly active role in international policy fora: Brazil is a member of the BRIC countries,[1] and three Latin American countries are in the world's premier economic forum, the G20 (Argentina, Brazil and Mexico).

Recent developments that have attracted international interest, and which merit scholarly attention, include the following:

- The LAC region has been acknowledged as pioneering innovative policy responses particularly relating to social assistance and social protection, conflict resolution, constitutional reform and human rights legislation. The documentation and analysis of these experiences are relevant to the international development policy community, as well as to the current concerns of the UK government, and other donors who focus on pro-poor growth, social inclusion and good governance.[2]

- Some countries of the region are leading developments in biofuel and biodiversity research, and are taking an active role in global discussions about environmental management. Indeed, the region's politicians increasingly recognise the significance of environmental security in

1 Brazil, Russia, India and China.

2 See the Department for International Development's ELLA programme report at: http://r4d.dfid.gov.uk/Project/60739/ (accessed 3 April 2012).

view of predicted climate change. They also acknowledge the need to engage with, and position their governments vis-à-vis multilateral environmental initiatives based on potential, either as large carbon-dependent economies (e.g. Brazil and Mexico), or as low carbon emitters vulnerable to climate change (e.g. the island states of the Caribbean).

- As a member of the European Union (EU), the UK is involved in a wide range of policy initiatives, trade links and multilateral policy initiatives which involve the LAC region. International recognition is growing of the evolving expertise, scholarship and research capacities of institutions in the region.[3] As a result, the UK is engaging in increasingly productive research exchanges and collaboration on a range of high-profile issues in such areas as climate control, anti-poverty programmes and biodiversity. Environmental concerns, particularly in Amazonia, have intensified research activities and collaboration between Brazil and the UK, and have stimulated student and public interest in the country.
- Latin America figures with increasing prominence in UK foreign policy considerations, especially regarding increased trade and investment. Foreign Secretary William Hague signalled this in his Canning Lecture of 2010, when he announced the end of what he referred to as the UK's diplomatic retreat from Latin America. Outlining the UK's historical and present-day relationship with the region, he regretted the fact that the UK's contribution to all international exports to Latin America then amounted to scarcely 1 per cent.[4] He continued by pointing out areas in which Latin America can play an increasing role in international cooperation: the great majority of its countries are democracies, which have introduced innovations in social policy and are making advances in tackling climate change. He then presented measures aimed at changing the poor relationship of the past: an increased diplomatic presence, increasing trade and investment in both directions and collaboration on tackling drugs and violence. He also emphasised the role of education, and specifically the British Council, wishing to 'see the UK as the partner of choice in education and culture, offering new

3 According to the *Times Higher Education* World University Rankings 2013, of the 400 top universities in the world in humanities and social science, four are in Latin America – Brazil (2), Chile and Mexico – whereas in 2009 there were none.

4 The full text of Secretary Hague's Canning House speech is available at: www.gov.uk/government/speeches/britain-and-latin-america-historic-friends-future-partners?view=Speech&id=23536682 (accessed 2 Feb. 2013).

English language skills to a wider audience and fostering knowledge sharing and creativity in arts and science.' In January 2012, he further reinforced those points in an interview on the eve of a visit to Brazil and in various speeches during that visit, describing Brazil as 'one of the emerging powers of the world', which he saw as sharing many of the UK's values.[5] That interview reiterated points made in a House of Commons Foreign Affairs Committee policy publication on UK–Brazil Relations in 2011,[6] which developed the main points of Hague's Canning House Lecture: increased trade and diplomacy, a stronger bilateral relationship with Brazil.

- In January 2013, Hugo Swire, the Foreign Office minister responsible for Latin America, wrote a blog post about the strengthening economic relationship between the UK and Latin America, seeing the latter as a growth market not to be ignored. He reported an 11 per cent increase in UK exports to the region (including the Caribbean) during the first 11 months of 2012, due in part to increases in the UK's diplomatic profile (specifically the opening of new embassies in El Salvador, Haiti and Paraguay, and a new Consulate-General in Recife).[7]

- In the case of Mexico, this new interest reflects the country's key economic and political role in the region, as a participant in the North American Free Trade Agreement (NAFTA), as the second largest economy in Latin America, and as a key G20 player. British interests in the country are underpinned by commercial links developed through the Trade Partners UK initiative, backed by the Department of Trade and Industry, its successor the Department of Business, Innovation and Skills, and the Foreign and Commonwealth Office (FCO), as well as the signing of a free-trade agreement between Mexico and the EU.[8]

- In the case of Brazil, this is evidenced by transformations over the past two decades, making the country the world's seventh biggest economy, and, as one of the BRIC group, helping to reshape the

5 www.politics.co.uk/comment-analysis/2012/01/20/william-hague-s-latin-aerica-speech-in-fullm (accessed 30 Jan. 2014).

6 www.publications.parliament.uk/pa/cm201012/cmselect/cmfaff/949/949.pdf (accessed 18 Feb. 2013).

7 http://blogs.fco.gov.uk/davidlidington/2013/01/25/why-latin-america-matters-to-britain/ (accessed 30 Jan. 2014).

8 www.politics.co.uk/comment-analysis/2012/01/20/william-hague-s-latin-aerica-speech-in-fullm (accessed 30 Jan. 2014).

global economic landscape.[9] Trade policies and market liberalisation have led to an unprecedented expansion of Brazil's trade and Foreign Direct Investment (FDI), and UK enterprises have led in taking advantage of the new opportunities. The UK government is also committed to improving trade links with Brazil.[10]

- Cultural and educational exchanges have also developed with the UK, though this tends to reflect Latin American interest in the UK rather than the other way round. For example, the activities of the Brazilian scholarly community have gained increasing international visibility over the last decade or so, 'competing on a global stage with long-standing research powerhouses such as the UK, Germany, France and the US'.[11] Education was specifically mentioned in a bulletin produced after Hague's visit to Brazil in January 2012, entitled 'UK and Brazil commit to developing enhanced foreign policy relationship', which affirmed the commitment to welcome up to 10,000 Brazilian students and researchers to 77 UK institutions until 2014 as part of the 'Science without Borders' programme.[12]
- In March 2011, the Deputy Prime Minister, Nick Clegg, led a delegation to Mexico, which included the Vice-Chancellors of six UK universities; Clegg laid great emphasis on promoting the 'education industry', which he described as a 'British success story', specifically talking of his hopes that UK universities might set up satellite operations abroad in countries such as Mexico.[13]
- Reflecting this positive environment, the Rt Hon Lord Howell of Guildford announced, in a speech delivered on 22 March 2012, that the British Council had trebled its budget for the region, investing in cultural exchanges, English language training and education.[14]

9 World Bank. Brazil Overview: www.worldbank.org/en/country/brazil/overview (accessed 10 Jan. 2014).

10 www.publications.parliament.uk/pa/cm201012/cmselect/cmfaff/949/949.pdf (accessed 10 Jan. 2014).

11 Department for Innovation, Universities and Skills (2013) *International Comparative Performance of the UK Research Base*. This report, produced by Elsevier is available at: www.gov.uk/government/uploads/system/uploads/attachment_data/file/263729/bis-13-1297-international-comparative-performance-of-the-UK-research-base-2013.pdf (accessed 30 Jan. 2014).

12 https://www.gov.uk/government/news/uk-and-brazil-commit-to-developing-enhanced-foreign-policy-relationship (accessed 28 Feb. 2013).

13 www.guardian.co.uk/business/2011/mar/28/nick-clegg-latin-america-business?INTCMP=SRCH (accessed 28 Feb. 2013).

14 See https://www.gov.uk/government/speeches/making-the-most-of-our-relations-with-latin-america (accessed 28 Feb. 2013).

What all this means therefore is that, in order to respond to and engage with these new developments, the UK needs to build on its strong tradition of scholarship about the LAC region and promote specialist knowledge, including essential language skills, in order to fully engage with the region.

Rationale

In the light of growing interest in the LAC region from academics, government, business and cultural institutions this report aims to:

a) identify changes in UK-based research in the region since the three previous national studies in 1965, 1996 and 2002.

b) analyse the prevailing patterns, trends, strengths and weaknesses of such research, as well as the patterns and trends both of the research funding underpinning it.

c) assess the challenges facing those engaging in such research.

It is hoped that this report will:

a) contribute to wider knowledge and a national discussion about the importance to the UK of LAC research, encouraging and enabling funding bodies, academic decision-makers, higher education institutions (hereafter called 'universities' in this report) and relevant subject associations to strengthen and develop such research, and also to contribute to a renewed awareness of the importance to the UK of area studies.

b) encourage and inform necessary discussions between the LAC research community and their relevant universities to protect and develop existing opportunities and infrastructure for LAC research.

Methodology

This report is based on research undertaken in 2009–10 and then 2012–13, on both occasions involving the collection of information using a range of relevant sources and methods, including a questionnaire, interviews with institutional representatives and individuals, and analysis of published reports and data.

Several challenges faced the conduct of a comprehensive review of the state of LAC research:

- Identifying the numbers of LAC scholars in the UK is not easy, since many of those conducting such research do not identify themselves formally as Latin Americanists or Caribbeanists, and are not actively involved in any of the three learned societies which cover research on, rather than in, the region. This is particularly true of social scientists, some of whom conduct international comparative research, not focused exclusively on LAC countries or others whose aim is to make a theoretical contribution, with the LAC country, region or city acting as a secondary case study.

- Outside the designated research-based centres (see below), no university departments focus exclusively on the LAC region. Official statistics from the Higher Education Statistics Agency (HESA) are therefore of limited value as they do not allow the identification of specific departments within universities focusing on LAC. Much research in this subject area will, however, take place in other departments (e.g. in culture, history, language, politics) and so could be reported to HESA within those relevant cost centres. This is a familiar problem with many disciplines – the data are not disaggregated at a low enough level to properly identify specific areas of research. Similarly, in recent research assessment exercises (RAEs), the research of the scholars in question has often been submitted for assessment to disciplinary-specific panels, making it difficult to obtain an overview of the size of the LAC research community and the quality and scope of its research. Again, this is often because of decisions taken within universities to submit an entire department to one panel, and not because the LAC research is not taking place.

- Because of this, many of the findings outlined below have necessarily relied heavily on interview data with some of those active in the field, however, this does of course limit the conclusions that can be drawn.

With these limitations in mind, the main sources were:

- The online *Handbook of Latin American and Caribbean Studies*, which provides data on teaching programmes, researchers' institutional and discipline affiliations, and the region and/or country specialisation of research being undertaken. It was originally created by the University of London's Institute of Latin American Studies and was subsequently developed and, as part of the data-gathering for this report, updated with funds from the British Academy Learned Societies scheme, channelled through the Joint Initiative for the Study of Latin America and the Caribbean. As an interactive internet portal, hosted on the ILAS website (www.ilas.sas.ac.uk), it is a dynamic website, so to ensure comparability of data, information presented in figures and tables was confined to 2009.

- Databases on the awards granted by research councils and funding bodies. The data was retrieved at various points between 2009 and 2013 compiled, analysed, and compared, as far as is allowed by the sources' very different and variably user-friendly forms of data retrieval. Changes in policies and funding schemes often make it difficult to track changes over time, in addition to which it is not always possible to disaggregate the data by geographical region.

- Three separate surveys were conducted by questionnaire. The first two were distributed, electronically (2009), through learned society membership lists and representatives on the Standing Conference of Directors of Centres of Latin American and Caribbean Studies. One was directed at individual academics and included questions on research profile, research funding, scholarly networks and publication strategies. A second was aimed at postgraduate students, with questions on research areas, sources of funding, networks and future careers. The two surveys together were completed by 48 academics and 37 postgraduates; although the response rate was disappointing, at approximately 10–20 per cent of these two groups nationally, it can still be argued that this represents a statistically significant sample.

- Later, in 2012–13, a new follow-up questionnaire was distributed to selected centres and departments, seeking updates on the previous information. It was emailed to 80 individuals connected with 37 UK universities, 41 of whom from 30 universities replied. The topics explored in the questionnaire were: the LAC research interests of the department concerned; the numbers of researchers involved; the disciplines involved; changes to the university structure affecting LAC research since 2009; internal and external funding since 2009; information on both undergraduate and postgraduate levels and courses, again since 2009.

- Membership lists obtained from the Society for Latin American Studies (SLAS), the Society for Caribbean Studies (SCS) and the Association of Hispanists of Great Britain and Ireland (AHGBI). These were consulted in 2009, as part of the initial data-gathering exercise.
- Interviews in person and by phone were conducted in 2009, with 77 individuals from within academia and relevant user organisations, with a view to capturing the variety of institutional and subjective perspectives and experiences within the field of LAC research.
- Selected public documents, reviewed for information on wider trends and to contextualise the significance of the research findings.

Since much LAC research falls into the category of 'area studies', this is the first context to consider here. Area studies were established in the UK during the Cold War, drawing largely on theoretical and methodological approaches in the social sciences, humanities and arts, with the aim of providing an understanding of defined geographic and sociocultural regions, often based on definitions originating from the colonial period. Research approaches in area studies have typically been comparative and either multidisciplinary, cross-disciplinary or interdisciplinary, usually requiring language skills where relevant to the designated geographical area. It is generally recognised by government agencies and academics alike that area studies can make a valuable contribution to informing the public and the government about relevant regions, not least because the interdisciplinary nature of the subject in each case allows for a greater understanding of the complexity of each society studied.[15]

Indeed, according to the Quality Assurance Agency for Higher Education (QAAHE), area studies 'enable students ... to acquire a unique depth and breadth of insight into the social, cultural and political dynamic of a region'.[16] They train graduates to enter the globalised job market where intercultural competences and relevant language skills are important, and prepare professionals for the important task of engaging with counterparts in foreign countries in an increasingly interdependent world.

15 For example, Goodman, Roger (ed.) (2005) *The Future of Interdisciplinary Area Studies in the UK: A Source Document*. Report of a workshop held in Oxford in December 2005.

16 Quality Assurance Agency for Higher Education (2008) 'Benchmark statement: area studies', available at: www.qaa.ac.uk/en/Publications/Documents/Subject-benchmark-statement-Area-studies.pdf (accessed 30 Jan. 2014).

The development of Latin American and Caribbean studies in the UK

What the above paragraphs imply is that the situation of LAC studies in the UK should first be understood in the light of the development and situation of area studies generally. This is not least because the original purpose of LAC studies some 50 years ago was fully concomitant with the overall value and purpose of area studies (outlined above). For the creation of a new subject, Latin American studies (the Caribbean was added much later) was clearly underpinned by the then government's awareness of the lack of knowledge about the region, particularly at a time of political change, when it became the focus of world attention. This resulted in the University Grants Committee (UGC) setting up a committee to report on Latin American studies. It ultimately published the Parry Report in 1965, which effectively led to the birth of 'Latin American studies'.[17]

One outcome of the Parry Report was the creation of five specialist centres for Latin American studies, known thereafter as 'Parry centres', at the Universities of Cambridge, Glasgow, Liverpool, London and Oxford. A further centre was established at Essex in 1968 (with Nuffield Foundation funds), specialising in Latin American politics. A system of postgraduate scholarships (known as Parry awards) was also established, which helped to create a generation of researchers across the country.

Although the University of London's Institute of Commonwealth Studies (ICwS) had existed since 1949, including within its remit the Anglophone Caribbean, Caribbean studies in the UK were further institutionalised nationally by the recommendations of the UGC through the establishment of the Centre for Caribbean Studies at the University of Warwick in 1984, with funding from the Leverhulme Trust and the Nuffield Foundation.

In 1996 an edited study, reviewing progress since 1965 in formal teaching programmes and research on Latin America, reported ten concentrations (within universities) of academic programmes and research activities. This attested to the successful fulfilment of the Parry Report objective of providing interdisciplinary teaching and research expertise on the region in institutions across the country. It also documented trends and contributions of British scholarship within different disciplines, noting its quality and breadth, and its relative strengths in areas ignored, until then, by its US counterpart, but

17 University Grants Committee (1965) *Report of the Committee on Latin American Studies* (London: HMSO).

identifying the relative weakness of its coverage of some of the region's larger countries, particularly Brazil.[18]

A smaller-scale and much less detailed report on undergraduate and taught postgraduate provision followed in 2002. It noted the development of masters provision beyond the Parry centres (often in individual region-specific modules on more general masters programmes, but including two new masters programmes in cultural studies) and the emergence of cultural studies as a growing discipline.[19] This report was paralleled by an article-length study of research on Latin America in the UK, which chronicled in great detail the growth of such research, identifying a healthy picture for some disciplines (politics, literature and culture, and anthropology and sociology), a worrying stagnation in some areas (notably history, given its past strength as one of the mainstays of the subject), and two weaknesses (economics and archaeology). It also identified several countries attracting a greater number of researchers: Chile, Argentina, Peru, Mexico and Brazil.[20]

This development has helped to foster, and also been reflected in, a shift in geographical definitions of the LAC region, from those that were essentially the product of historical and imaginative constructs derived from the colonial period – subsequently perpetuated by the prevailing view that a Latin American identity has been forged in opposition to the United States,[21] – to various new conceptual reconfigurations (such as the 'Greater Caribbean' or 'Pan-Caribbeanism'). This has revealed an ongoing debate within the academic community about such definitions and also the intellectual impact of, and responses to, the processes of globalisation, migration, trade, political integration and growing environmental concern, thus broadening conceptual boundaries.

International comparisons are of some relevance here. In the United States, federal provision (Title VI) is specifically designated for centres of excellence of area studies to support the development of their research programmes. These were established after the Second World War, when the need for relevant expertise was explicitly linked to the strengthening of the nation's security

18 Victor Bulmer-Thomas (ed.) (1996) *Thirty Years of Latin American Studies in the United Kingdom 1965–1995* (London: Institute of Latin American Studies).

19 Nikki Craske and Lewis Taylor (2002) *Latin American Studies in the UK* (Southampton: Subject Centre for Languages, Linguistics and Area Studies).

20 Nikki Craske and David Lehmann (2002) 'Fifty years of research in Latin American Studies in the UK', *European Review of Latin American and Caribbean Studies*, Amsterdam, no. 72, April, pp. 61–80.

21 James Dunkerley (2004) *Dreaming of Freedom in the Americas. Four Minds and a Name* (London: Institute for the Study of the Americas).

and economic competitiveness.[22] Bipartisan support for this programme was reiterated following the September 2001 terrorist attacks on the World Trade Centre, when the government asserted the importance of knowledge of, and expertise in, distinct world regions.[23] Equally, in Germany, the government has launched a four-year funding programme totalling 40 million euros (2009–13), with the aim of enabling area studies to survive on a sustainable basis.

New developments affecting Latin American and Caribbean studies

Since 1996, there have been significant developments which generate opportunities and challenges to the UK-based LAC research community.

On the plus side:

- Recent decades have seen some growth in public interest in the region, stimulated by increased travel and television coverage (albeit largely evidenced by the popularity of Latin American culture or the popularity of the region as a destination for 'gap-year' visits).
- The Latin American population in the UK has also increased dramatically since the 1970s; there are now an estimated one million people of Latin American ancestry,[24] predominantly Brazilians, Colombians, Ecuadorians and Peruvians, constituting one of the fastest-growing immigrant communities in the UK.[25] This could lead to an increased demand for region-specific offerings at UK universities in the coming years, although there is as yet no proven correlation between ethnic origin of immigrant-based communities and the regional or cultural focus of university study.
- The high cost of living to study in Europe (during the 'year abroad'), as opposed to study outside Europe, has led to a detectable tendency for those studying Spanish (in some form or other) at university to opt for Latin America, rather than Spain. Recent questionnaire responses

22 US Department of Education, Office of International and Foreign Language Education, at: www.ed.gov/about/offices/list/ope/iegps (accessed 10 Jan. 2014).

23 www.nhalliance.org/advocacy/funding-priorities/international-education-programs-fy2013.shtml (accessed 10 Jan. 2014).

24 Based on figures provided by embassies and community organisations. For data on Latin Americans in London see: www.geog.qmul.ac.uk/latinamericansinlondon/index.html (accessed 22 Sep. 2013).

25 http://news.bbc.co.uk/1/shared/spl/hi/uk/05/born_abroad/countries/html/south_america.stm (accessed 30 Jan. 2014).

suggest that despite those costs, such interest has not declined as much as might have been expected.

However, on the negative side:

- The structural and financial reorganisation within universities has threatened the existence of some small departments or units and interdisciplinary centres.[26] Research assessment processes, especially the 2008 RAE, to be discussed below, have also led in the past to an increased organisation of units according to the logic of discipline submissions. This has resulted in a perception among some scholars that interdisciplinary work is downgraded and dissuaded some academics from undertaking interdisciplinary or multidisciplinary research, despite policymakers' and funding bodies' formal encouragement of such work.[27]

- The guidelines for the 2014 Research Excellence Framework (REF), the RAE's successor, do show a greater awareness of this tendency by encouraging researchers to submit interdisciplinary and multidisciplinary work for assessment, and also by writing this into the panels' criteria.

- It is worth noting that funding decisions taken after RAE 2008 have sometimes seen science, technology, engineering and mathematics (STEM) subjects receive additional investment. This may well be inevitable, given that the subjects are more expensive, require significant capital investment and are often run by means of large teams and external funding – these disciplines therefore tend to have more financial support associated with them. However, it is a concern that the focus on these subjects detracts from the importance of the arts, humanities and social sciences (AHSS), despite outstanding performances and improvements. The challenge for the AHSS communities is to ensure that the powerful arguments to be made in favour of investing in those disciplines are heard by those with influence (e.g. national governments and funding organisations).

- Despite the fact that Spanish has increased in popularity at school level, UK-educated researchers generally lack adequate linguistic competence

26 Elizabeth Bird (2001) 'Disciplining the interdisciplinary: radicalism and the academic curriculum', *British Journal of Sociology of Education*, vol. 2, no. 4, pp. 464–78.

27 *Times Higher Education* (2008) 'REF could penalise those working across disciplines', 2 Oct.; also see Jonathan Levitt and Mike Thelwall (2008) 'Is multi-disciplinary research more highly cited? A macro-level study', *Journal of the American Society for Information Science and Technology*, vol. 59, no. 12, pp. 1973–84.

for deep academic research on a Spanish-speaking country. This compares badly with the numbers of researchers from other countries with relevant language skills[28] and is clearly related to growing evidence of, and concern about, the falling demand for language study and linguistic competence within the UK. This has generated successive national reports, all expressing growing disquiet at the decline and its implications. In 2009, the Worton Report, commissioned by the Higher Education Funding Council for England (HEFCE),[29] highlighted the sharp decline in language learning in higher education, following the government's decision in 2002 to make study of the subject in schools optional after the age of 14. The report made an explicit link with area studies, suggesting that boosting the latter – and specifically the study of Latin America – might have the effect of stimulating language study once again and might in turn be regenerated by such a revival. As part of a dedicated programme to address the UK's language deficit, the British Academy published a State of the Nation report in 2013, providing strong evidence that the UK is suffering from this growing deficit at a time when global demand is expanding.[30] The report makes the case for bridging the gap between the education and employment sectors – arguing that a weak supply of language skills in the job market is pushing down demand, creating a vicious circle of monolingualism. More recently, the Academy's report, *Lost for Words: the Need for Languages in UK Diplomacy and Security*, argues that persistent deficits in these skills threaten the UK's future capacity for influence.[31]

28 The British Academy (2009) 'Language matters: a position paper' (London: The British Academy), available at: www.britac.ac.uk/policy/language-matters.cfm (accessed 30 Jan. 2014).

29 Michael Worton (2009) 'Review of modern foreign languages provision in higher education in England' (London: HEFCE), available at: www.britac.ac.uk/policy/language-matters.cfm (accessed 30 Jan. 2014).

30 The British Academy (2013) 'Languages: the state of the nation' (London: The British Academy), available at: www.britac.ac.uk/policy/State_of_the_Nation_2013.cfm (accessed 30 Jan. 2014).

31 The British Academy (2013) 'Lost for words: the need for languages in UK diplomacy and security' (London: The British Academy), available at: www.britac.ac.uk/policy/Lost_For_Words.cfm (accessed 30 Jan. 2014).

Scope and patterns of research on Latin America and the Caribbean in the UK

Size and composition of the research community[32]

- According to the data available, more researchers appear to be actively working on the LAC region than ever before (see Table 1). In 2009, there were around 570 researchers in AHSS, compared to approximately 360 in 1997, and they were located in about two-thirds of UK universities.

- In the view of those interviewed the scale of the increase since 2003 is likely to be slightly exaggerated, particularly since during the same period the number of full-time academic staff in UK universities fell slightly.[33] Most likely the apparent increase is due to a combination of under-reporting in 2003 (especially in comparison with the 1997 figures) with the more intensive search for specialists outside traditional departments conducted as part of this report. However, it is worth noting (as this report indicated earlier) that the statistics gathered draw on the *Handbook of Latin American and Caribbean Studies in the UK*, which relies on scholars' self-identification as Latin Americanists or Caribbeanists. It is known that more people conduct research on Latin America, particularly in the social sciences, who would not regard themselves as regional specialists. Hence, it seems likely that the numbers researching on LAC are greater than these figures might suggest.

- Of the academics, about 20 per cent (111) research the Caribbean exclusively or combine such research with work on other areas or countries of the wider region; this compares with 10 per cent (41) in 1997. Therefore, it seems that research on the Caribbean is being carried out by a growing number of UK-based researchers.

32 Further to the caveat indicated earlier in this report concerning the reliability of the *Handbook* data, it should be noted here that, where the figures referred to are confirmed by other sources of information, the report treats them with more confidence. Equally, the report makes it clear when other evidence appears to contradict the figures given.

33 HESA statistics are available at: www.hesa.ac.uk/index.php?option=com_datatables&Itemid=121&task=show_category&catdex=2 (accessed 1 May 2013).

Table 1. Approximate number of those engaging in LAC research in the UK

Year	Number of academics	Number of doctoral students	Total	Number of universities*
2009	569	157	726	91
2003	294	197	419	59
1997	359	330	689	75

Sources: *Handbook of Latin American and Caribbean Studies in the UK* (1997, 2003), Institute of Latin American Studies. The original print versions have been made available in searchable format, originally at: //handbook.americas.sas.ac.uk (accessed 12 Oct. 2009), and now at: http://ilas.sas.ac.uk/portal (accessed 25 Jan. 2014). The report will cite the up-to-date address from this point, but with the original date of access.

*Here, the term 'universities' includes 'universities' and 'university colleges'. The institutions which comprise the federal organisations of the University of London and the University of Wales are counted as 12 and four separate institutions.

- Table 1 indicates that, despite the increased number of academics actively researching on the region, the amount of doctoral theses in progress in UK universities appears to have fallen by 50 per cent since 1997. Since such a reduction is not reflected in other evidence, notably in the number of Arts and Humanities Research Council (AHRC) and Economic and Social Research Council (ESRC) studentships discussed below, it is likely that it results from: i) under-reporting by students themselves; and ii) supervision of postgraduates working on the region by discipline specialists who do not research exclusively on LAC and who have thus not been identified by the *Handbook*.

- The doctoral student population seems increasingly to be of Latin American origin or descent. Of those registered with Postgraduates in Latin American Studies (PILAS) in 2009, almost half came from Latin America, Portugal or Spain. Survey responses suggest that the continuing practice within UK doctoral study to engage in research from the outset (rather than after an obligatory taught programme) has a high premium in Latin America, and is attractive in providing would-be Latin American doctoral students with an opportunity to gain comparative and regional expertise which is unavailable in their own country.

- Regional specialists are found in universities across all academic grades in the proportions illustrated in Figure 1. Professors appear to be well represented, with one in four academics holding chairs. This would seem to reflect a success story for the subject, since many of those with such a title belong to the generation that was either trained in the Parry centres or benefited from Parry awards. Certainly, these people seem to have played active roles within their own institutions, or nationally (on committees and funding panels, and in learned societies). However, this concentration at the top of the scale also implies a potential challenge for the subject, as many now approach retirement. That said, however, one in three researchers on the region are either Readers or Senior/Principal Lecturers, suggesting that a new generation of regional specialists is approaching seniority. Nevertheless, interview data indicate that staff do not consider institutional changes and policies to be conducive to the appointment of area studies specialists to vacant posts.

Figure 1. Percentages of different grades of staff employed by UK universities and carrying out LAC research in 2009

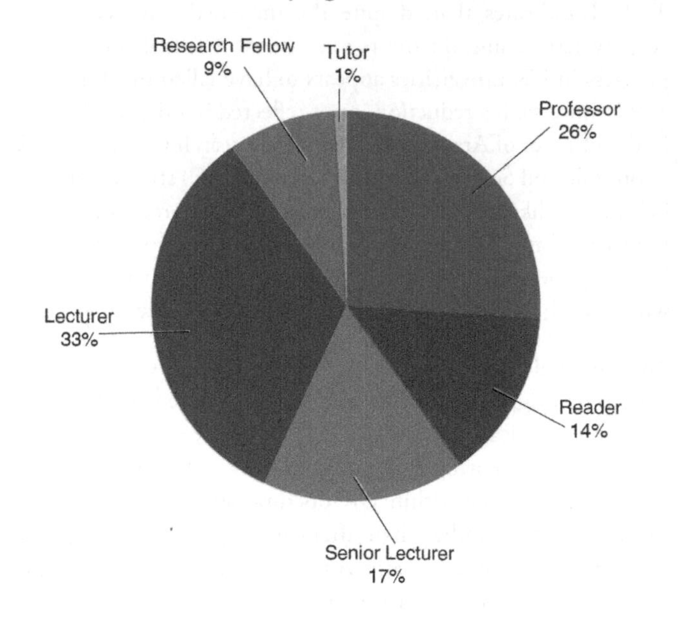

Source: *Handbook of Latin American and Caribbean Studies in the UK*, at: http://ilas.sas.ac.uk/portal (accessed 12 Oct. 2009).

The national origin and ethnicity of those researching on the region in the UK are increasingly diverse. One-third of the 85 survey respondents originated from other European countries, the United States or Latin America; many were trained abroad but some completed doctoral study in the UK. While this reflects both the increased global mobility of academics and graduate students, and wider transnational migration patterns, it may also reflect the linguistic limitations of UK-educated students noted earlier in the report.

Institutional affiliations and research concentrations

UK-based LAC researchers work in various concentrations and levels of organisation within universities, but are also employed in institutions beyond academia. They are found in the following broad configurations:

A. The most significant concentrations occur in those universities with teaching programmes that include clusters of modules or specific courses on the region, demanding specialist provision. They can be found in two types of universities:

   i) Those which have established programmes and centres relating to Latin America and/or the Caribbean.

      - Fourteen institutions were offering a total of 33 undergraduate programmes in Latin American studies in 2013, though the majority were combined with Hispanic and Portuguese studies, and only one was offering a single honours degree.[34] No single honours undergraduate degree in Caribbean studies is available, but it is offered at Warwick and Liverpool as part of degrees in Comparative American studies.

      - In 2009 the *Handbook* recorded that 25 full masters programmes were being offered, shared by 16 institutions, two of them relating specifically to the Caribbean.[35] Since then the number of masters courses dedicated exclusively to Latin American or Caribbean studies has declined to 18, though masters degrees in other disciplines often offer pathways enabling a degree of specialisation in the region.

   Of these institutions, the Institute of Latin American Studies (ILAS) at the School of Advanced Study, University of London, has a distinctive role, in that it has a national remit from HEFCE to 'promote and

34 www.ucas.ac.uk/students/coursesearch/2013searcheu/ (accessed 11 May 2013), now http://search.ucas.com/.

35 *Handbook of Latin American and Caribbean Studies* (accessed 12 Oct. 2009).

facilitate research' on LAC. The Institute maintains a vibrant programme of seminars, workshops and conferences on the LAC region, which attract speakers and members of the public from across the UK and beyond. Survey interviewees have confirmed ILAS's value as a focal point of exchange for researchers and for both private and public sectors, including policymaking communities. Between 2004–12, ILAS and the Institute of United States Studies constituted the Institute for the Study of the Americas, which offered a large social science postgraduate teaching programme focusing on globalisation, development and politics. This has since moved to the UCL Institute of the Americas.

In addition, two dedicated centres for the study of Latin America focus on more specialist aspects: the long-established University of St Andrews Centre for Indigenous American Studies and Exchange, and the University of Manchester's Centre for Latin American and Caribbean Studies (until 2009, the Centre for Latin American Cultural Studies), although it no longer runs masters courses. In 2002, the Caribbean Studies Centre was established in London Metropolitan University, but subsequently suffered seriously in LMU's difficult financial situation in 2009 and has since closed.

Among this group of universities are four with small country-specific centres, focusing on Brazil (King's College London and Oxford), Cuba (Nottingham) and Mexico (Southampton).

ii) Those which offer combined degrees with a Latin American or Caribbean component.

- Apart from those institutions mentioned which offer combined degrees in LAC studies, most of the rest display a lower level of institutional support, but offer combinations under the rubric of language, social science or humanities disciplines, or broader programmes such as cultural and development studies.

- In some of these academics from different departments have created informal but active research groups, as in the cases of Newcastle's Americas Study Group, Edinburgh's Caribbean and Latin American Research group, and a similar group in Glasgow. These groupings organise activities on their campuses and cater for pragmatic research needs, such as sharing research contacts, which are particularly valued by research students and early career scholars. Where numbers are significantly large, researchers have also developed collaborative research projects.

The highest concentrations of researchers on the region (currently totalling 16 institutions) are represented within the Standing Conference of Centres of Latin American and Caribbean Studies. In 2012 it included Aberystwyth, Bristol, Cambridge, Essex, ILAS, King's College London, Liverpool, Oxford, Manchester, Newcastle, Nottingham, Portsmouth, Southampton, Stirling, St Andrews, Swansea, UCL Institute for the Americas and Warwick. This number constitutes both a growth since 1996, when only ten institutions were represented,[36] and a dispersion of LAC scholarship.

The incidence of these clusters is not necessarily the consequence of institutional commitments to support research on the region since, in some cases, concentrations of regional expertise have developed on a more ad hoc basis within particular departments or as a result of a department's conscious specialisation strategy (e.g. anthropology at Manchester), often in support of individual endeavour or success.

B. The second category is other institutions in which LAC specialists undertake research without teaching obligations:

- Prominent among this group are those working at the Royal Institute of International Affairs, Development Studies Institute (DESTIN), now the Department for International Development (DFID) at the London School of Economics (LSE), the Brooks World Poverty Institute (Manchester), the Institute for Development Studies (Sussex), the Overseas Development Institute and the International Institute for Environment and Development. This category also includes those researchers employed in public institutions, such as museums and galleries.
- These researchers may also act as supervisors for doctoral students. Indeed, research councils now facilitate this through the provision of Collaborative Doctoral Awards, intended to encourage and develop collaboration and partnerships between university departments and non-academic organisations and businesses.

36 New additions to the membership between 1997 and 2012 were: Aberystwyth, Bristol, King's College London, Manchester, Newcastle, Nottingham, Southampton and Stirling, while Bradford and Glasgow ceased to be members.

C. The final category comprises universities with no specific organised or defined interest in the region, where lone academics pursue their LAC research interests without any corresponding teaching responsibilities relating to their geographical area of expertise.

Shifting institutional commitments to LAC research

Across all of these institutions various trends in support for research on the region can be identified. The scenario is dynamic: activities are contracting in some locations, but expanding in others. The following scenarios demonstrate how the institutional landscape of LAC research is being transformed in the UK.

- Interviews with representatives from non-university public sector institutions (e.g. Tate Gallery, British Museum, Liverpool Maritime Museum, National Archives, the British Library) indicated that over the last decade such institutions have steadily increased the level of funding and staff recruitment for LAC research-related activities. This is in response to the demand for them to become more global in outlook and cater for growing public interest in the region, and is often done in close collaboration with researchers from universities.

- Over the years universities have not unsurprisingly changed priorities. The many reasons for this include institutional reorganisation and funding priorities, research evaluation systems, student demand, journals, peer review systems and the efforts of researchers themselves to protect or create productive research environments in their institutions. Of the original Parry centres, Cambridge, Oxford, and the Institute for Latin American Studies are still in existence, albeit with some changes, while the long-established centres at Essex and Warwick also continue. The Parry centre at Glasgow closed in 1997 and the Institute for Latin American Studies at Liverpool ceased to be a separate entity in 2005 when its staff members were absorbed into the School of Cultures, Languages and Area Studies (SOCLAS). At Oxford and Liverpool senior posts vacated by LAC researchers have not been filled.

- On the other hand, centres have emerged in other universities in response to high student demand for regionally focused modules and in recognition of the benefits accruing from a centre organised around a teaching programme which generates synergies for scholarly exchange, interdepartmental cooperation and collaborative research endeavours. In one such case, researchers based in several departments (modern languages, politics and international relations) at the Swansea University obtained Senate approval for an interdisciplinary American programme and a research centre in 2010. However, in other universities, plans to extend or establish interdisciplinary and cross-departmental regional programmes have been derailed by institutional restructuring and budget considerations.

- Interviews with LAC scholars indicated that one of the most significant developments since the 1990s has been the emergence of many foci of regional expertise within departments of Spanish/Hispanic and/or Portuguese studies, or in schools of modern (or European) languages and cultures. They revealed that a small but apparently rising number of historians and social scientists now work in departments that were previously dominated by the humanities, and especially literary studies. This trend, indeed, has increased the movement within language departments away from traditional 'literature-based' approaches to language study towards a growing emphasis on cultural studies. In part, this transition has been driven by the relative decline in the numbers of students interested in literature-focused courses, but also by the growth and popularity of cultural studies as an area of specialisation.

Scholarly networks

In addition to the rising levels of LAC researchers, there has been a noticeable increase in regional academic networks and activities, confirming the vitality of the research community working on the region. These include:

1. Latin Americanist and Caribbeanist-related membership organisations

These have proliferated, facilitated by the ease of internet communications. They offer regional, sub-regional or country specialists productive fora for scholarly exchange, and are evidently highly valued by all researchers, especially given changing and less predictable institutional support for such research.

a) National organisations

Most of the UK's LAC researchers are members of at least one of the main relevant organisations, specifically: the Society for Latin American Studies (SLAS), the Society for Caribbean Studies (SCS) and the Association of Hispanists of Great Britain and Ireland (AHGBI). In fact there is considerable cross-membership, with many scholars belonging to more than one of them.

The SLAS (with around 400 UK-based members, including postgraduate researchers) is the largest organisation in Europe of its kind, attracting membership from overseas, particularly from the Netherlands, but also from the United States and Latin America, many of whom come to its annual conferences. These conferences attract around 150–200 participants, with around 30–40 panels. The Society also sponsors an affiliated organisation for postgraduates, Postgraduates in Latin American Studies (PILAS), with its own annual conference. The SLAS also constitutes a valuable source of small-scale funding to support postgraduate fieldwork in Latin America.

The SCS (with 160 UK-based members, including academics and postgraduates) also includes researchers from the Caribbean, continental Europe, Canada and the United States, many of whom also attend its annual conference.

The AHGBI traditionally focuses on Iberian studies, but its membership (including lecturing staff, postgraduates and corresponding members) includes about 150 researching on Latin America, accounting for an estimated one-third of all Hispanic studies academics in lecturing or research posts. The Association's membership and conferences tend to focus on literary and cultural studies research.

These organisations' annual conferences are the primary fora for scholarly exchanges and contacts between the relevant specialists; they are particularly valued by postgraduates whose supervisors are not regional specialists, by younger researchers, and by those who work in universities where there is no established regional programme. Non-academics, government officials, professionals, representatives of NGOs and other independent specialists also attend the SLAS and SCS conferences, enabling exchange between the academic and policy and practitioner communities.

Below this level, many researchers also participate in country-specific networks, with their own regular events.

Beyond these larger organisations, researchers also typically attend the professional conferences of their own discipline subject areas.

b) International organisations

i) The International Congress of Americanists (ICA) is the longest standing conference dedicated to Latin American studies. It has been convened uninterruptedly since it was first held, in 1875, in Nancy, France, with venues alternating between the Americas and Europe. It meets every three years and attracts several thousand participants, including many from the UK.

ii) United States-based organisations – many UK-based LAC researchers are also members of the Latin American Studies Association (LASA). In fact, interviews indicated that some British LAC researchers prefer to attend LASA annual conferences, rather than SLAS or SCS ones, as a way of showcasing their work more widely and of networking effectively with contemporaries from the region and the United States, although securing funds to attend meetings is often difficult.

iii) European associations – some LAC researchers are active members of European-wide associations, and value the importance of increased contacts with researchers in Europe, especially from Spain, Portugal and France. These associations typically cater for more focused academic interests, and include discipline-based societies (e.g. the Association of European Historians of Latin America) and country-specific organisations (e.g. the European Brazilianist Association). There is clearly scope within the Bologna process to expand collaboration between mainland European and UK LAC centres.

Although many UK-based LAC researchers prioritise collaboration and exchanges with colleagues in the region (and the United States) above links with those based in Europe, the strengthening of research and teaching programmes on LAC with other European countries highlights the significance of this as an area for development. The SLAS is a member of Consejo Europeo de Investigaciones Sociales sobre América Latina (CEISAL), a network that brings together institutes and centres of Latin American studies in Europe, but interviews suggested that so far scholars from the UK have not been actively involved in the organisation or its conferences.

From an EU perspective, the European Commission announced its new International Cooperation Communication in September 2012. Horizon 2020, the EU's research and innovation programme for 2014–20 will be open to participants worldwide but will restrict the funding available to countries considered as having become 'equal' partners, such as Brazil. Furthermore, in the 2013 Work Programme for the Social Science and Humanities Theme under FP7's Cooperation Pillar there was a call for establishing a 'transatlantic social sciences and humanities platform', which will step up international cooperation between research programmes and enhance networking of researchers.

2. Conferences held in the region

A few researchers attend conferences in the region. Brazilianists, for example, attend the Brazilian Studies Association's key annual international event. This Association was established in the early 1990s with a global membership of around 900. Others attend conferences such as those held by the Caribbean Studies Association, the Society for the Anthropology of Lowland South America (SALSA), the Conference of Latin Americanist Geographers and Asociación de Cientistas (sic) Sociales de la Religión en el Mercosur.

3. Representation of LAC studies in national fora

Beyond the institutional networks and subject associations, the prime national forum for LAC studies is the Standing Conference of Centres of Latin American and Caribbean Studies. The chair has, by consensus, taken on the role of pursuing and representing the interests of the many centres of Latin American and/or Caribbean studies in discussions with national decision-makers in government and funding councils.

In response to the need to promote and defend the integrity of area studies programmes and interdisciplinary research, representatives of the area studies academic community (including the SLAS and the SCS) established the UK Council for Area Studies Associations (UKCASA) in 2004, as the equivalent of a subject association for area studies, with the aim of providing a channel for direct contact with government and higher education funding bodies.

4. The Joint Initiative for the Study of Latin America and the Caribbean (JISLAC)

This body was created in 2007 by the SLAS, the SCS and the Standing Conference of Centres of Latin American Studies, and was funded until 2012 by the British Academy's Learned Societies programme. It was established to support the development of LAC studies in the UK, through the updating and development of the *Handbook*, a programme of small postdoctoral research grants (within a wider thematic programme) and a five-year programme of eight annual regional seminars throughout the UK. The latter especially built on and supported the existing and successful SCS seminar initiative, 'Caribbean research seminar series in the North'. The JISLAC programme generated local networks and an enthusiastic response. As part of its national research support and facilitation mission, ILAS now offers some support for the regional seminars.

In addition to the above organisations, a number of internet networks provide information and links for those studying and researching Latin American themes. The most notable is the LATAM-INFO service, which supplies up-to-date information about events of interest to the LAC academic community both within and beyond the universities.

Discipline concentrations

This section has been based substantially on *Handbook* data. Perhaps more than any other part of the report, it should be treated with caution because of its dynamic quality and its reliance on academics' self-identification. Nonetheless, the figures do seem to suggest some broad patterns and trends in the scale and scope of the different subjects within LAC studies, which accord with the perceptions of senior scholars in the field and its subject associations.

In particular, the following patterns stand out:

- Cultural studies have expanded to become a significant and distinct area of LAC research and studies. This has been encouraged by student demand (at undergraduate and postgraduate levels) leading to staff appointments, and also by the trend toward interdisciplinarity in humanities teaching and research which has encouraged former literary specialists and historians to transmute into specialists in cultural studies. As indicated in Table 2, there are now more academics who cite 'literature and culture' as their discipline than any other category. However, this trend is not reflected in the number of theses being conducted in the field (Table 3), perhaps because of the lack of funding to pursue PhD research in this subject area or because cultural studies are now also supervised in other disciplines. It remains to be seen what the impact of the rise in student fees and the reduction in direct HEFCE grants for teaching in the arts and humanities will have on recruitment.

  Interviews with academics revealed mixed responses to this trend. Some feel the expansion has brought new methodologies, new perspectives and a new theoretical flexibility to research on the region, helping to secure the future of Latin American studies, especially in languages departments. However, others fear that, as cultural studies expand, LAC research will be perceived as being unable to address key and social, political and economic issues and developments that are currently of increasing international interest. This seems unlikely, given that the number of academics in social science fields, especially politics and international relations, has generally increased or at least remained stable between 1997 and 2009 (Table 2).

- Other subjects (sometimes because of their relationship with cultural studies) – notably anthropology, art history and history – are all reported to be enjoying either steady growth or maintaining their existing position in respect of staff and student levels.

- A reduction in the number of researchers working on the region in economics seems to have occurred, such that the economics of Latin America is now taught as a specialist subject in very few institutions. Although it appears that more researchers are working in politics and international relations, the number of theses being written in this field has fallen. These trends may largely be explained by the prevailing theoretical paradigms within both disciplines, which have for the last two decades been dominated by empirical approaches including econometric and rational choice modelling. Analysis of the social and cultural contexts of institutions and political processes (once a staple of LAC research) seems currently not to be privileged within either political science or economics as general disciplines. Within economics, econometrics prevails and, as with political science, little premium is placed on contextualising analysis in relation to social and cultural phenomena.

Region and country focus

LAC-focused research covers a range of countries, with the following notable characteristics:

- Only a few countries were identified in the *Handbook* as being the subject of research by more than 40 researchers (including academics and doctoral students): Brazil (100), Mexico (83), Argentina (57), Cuba (43), Peru (41) and Colombia (40).
- With the closure of the Oxford Brazil Centre in 2007, only one Brazil-focused research institute exists (at King's College London). Nevertheless, research on Brazil appears to be an expanding area: in 2009, 85 academics registered it as a country of specialist research compared with 39 in 2003. Interviews suggested that this has been encouraged by Brazil's status as a rising power and, as discussed below, new collaborations between UK and Brazilian universities facilitated by funding from Brazil and UK research councils.
- This study has identified a widespread view that, given the rising significance of Brazil, the new funding initiatives of the research councils, opportunities to expand collaborative links between Brazilian and UK academic institutions (see below), and the emerging bilateral economic relationship, there is now a compelling case for expanding the UK's research capacity on the country.
- Although research on the Caribbean has expanded, it is still relatively sparse and is dominated by research on the Anglophone countries, followed by those working on the Hispanic areas. Research on the Francophone or Dutch-speaking Caribbean seems to attract only a handful of scholars to each area, the former usually found in French studies departments. Cuba, by contrast, is well-represented as a country

Table 2. Number of academics working in LAC studies in different disciplines

Year	Anthropology	Archaeology	Art history	Economic history	Economics	Geography	History	Literature & culture	Politics & IR	Sociology
1997	26	2	3	7	29	50	58	110	48	48
2009	44	12	17	5	34	43	86	157	93	40

Source: *Handbook of Latin American and Caribbean Studies in the UK*, at: http://ilas.sas.ac.uk/portal (accessed 12 Oct. 2009).

Table 3. Number of theses being written, according to disciplines

Year	Anthropology	Archaeology	Art history	Economic history	Economics	Geography	History	Literature & culture	Politics & IR	Sociology
1997	37	8	11	8	36	20	33	91	71	40
2003	23	2		4	7	29	34	61	37	13
2009	30		11	2	22	19	18	15	29	10

Source: *Handbook of Latin American and Caribbean Studies in the UK*, at: http://ilas.sas.ac.uk/portal (accessed 12 Oct. 2009).

of specialist interest, perhaps reflecting the continuing impact of Cuba's particular history and political significance when Latin American studies took off in the 1960s.

Research quality

There are many indicators of the high reputation which UK-based LAC research continues to earn:

- Survey responses and interviews for this report suggested that many LAC researchers, particularly in the social sciences, are regularly consulted by UK national agencies and government departments (e.g. DFID, FCO), as well as overseas governments, multilateral agencies, international organisations, commercial operations and the media. This attests to the high value non-academic entities place on the quality, relevance and depth of the expertise they consult in this way. The evidence also suggested that UK researchers are often cited in the non-academic literature on, and in, the region.
- The editors of both of the UK's main academic journals in the field, the *Journal of Latin American Studies* and *Bulletin of Latin American Research*, report that over recent years submissions by UK-based

Figure 2. Numbers of academics and doctoral students researching different countries in the LAC region in 2009

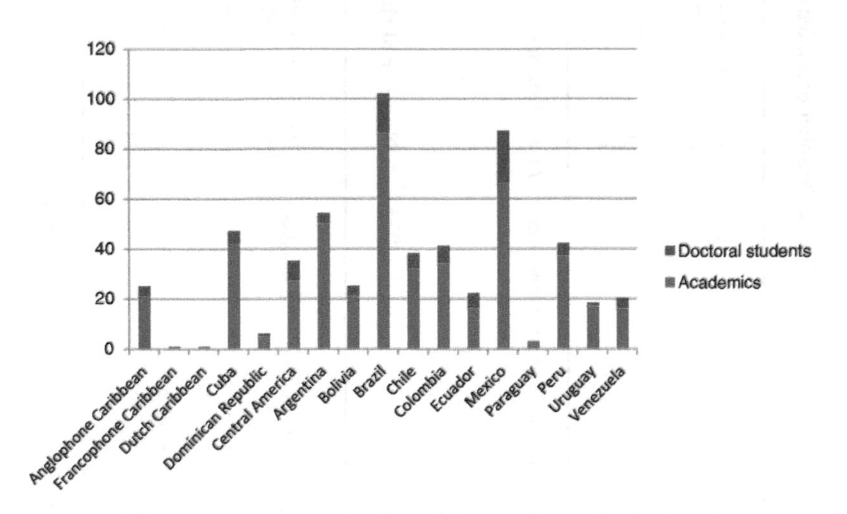

Source: *Handbook of Latin American and Caribbean Studies in the UK* (2009), at: http://ilas.sas.ac.uk/portal (accessed 12 Oct. 2009).

scholars are of a consistently high quality, with high acceptance rates, although there may be fewer UK submissions to the *Journal* than from the United States and Latin America. The impact factor of the *Journal of Latin American Studies* in 2011 was 0.54, which was higher than the main dedicated Latin American social science journals in the US.[37] An international strategic review of the *Journal* by Cambridge University Press in 2012 concluded that it was the premier journal in the field.

- Survey responses suggested that overseas students are attracted by the interdisciplinary and regional, or comparative, approaches of the UK's postgraduate and research degree programmes in LAC studies. UK doctorates are highly esteemed and gain the holders prestige when they return to work in their countries of origin.

- However, competition from other countries for these students has been intense. In 2012 the Mexican national funding agency, CONACYT, was supporting 4,036 postgraduates studying overseas (both PhDs and masters), of which 20.6 per cent were in the UK, 26.5 per cent in the US and 15.5 per cent in Spain.38 The recent growth in some Latin American economies has enabled greater priority to be afforded to education. Brazil's CAPES and CNPq joint programme, 'Science without Borders', now aims to send 10,000 students to the UK over four years beginning in September 2012, although this figure encompasses both undergraduates and postgraduates and, with the exception of the creative industries, focuses on the sciences.39 Table 4 shows that the number studying humanities and social science subjects has increased by about 20 per cent since 2007, while the rather uneven pattern of enrolment suggests that shifts in priorities and policies and the availability of LAC government funding play a particularly significant role.

37 In 2011 the impact factors for the *Latin American Research Review* and *Latin American Perspectives* were 0.187 and 0.337 respectively.

38 Of this number 40% were to study humanities or social sciences subjects.

39 CAPES is Brazil's Federal Agency for the Support and Evaluation of Graduate Education and CNPq is its National Council for Scientific and Technological Development. Science without Borders UK information is available at: http://sciencewithoutborders.international.ac.uk/about.aspx (accessed 2 May 2013).

Table 4. Number of postgraduates from selected LAC countries on taught and research humanities and social sciences courses in the UK

Country	2007/08	2008/09	2009/10	2010/11	2011/12
Argentina	128	115	91	114	94
Brazil	506	540	557	532	560
Chile	199	200	280	309	388
Colombia	217	290	366	388	408
Ecuador	24	19	50	22	39
Jamaica	141	106	223	67	63
Mexico	509	491	498	523	563
Peru	90	99	110	117	70
Trinidad & Tobago	169	193	219	206	181
Total	**1983**	**2053**	**2394**	**2278**	**2366**

Source: Higher Education Information Database for Institutions, Higher Education Statistics Agency at: www.heidi.ac.uk (accessed 16 May 2013).

Information resources and access to archives

Library holdings and other collections have developed within many institutions during the last 40 years as LAC programmes have proliferated. Those that follow represent significant national, and even international, assets:

- The British Library is the official repository for publications, including for the 30-strong Caribbean Publishers Network for the Anglophone Caribbean. In addition to a budget to purchase secondary literature and to ensure coverage of all the countries of the region, it also purchases some primary 'social' material, including Brazil street literature. Outreach activities from within the Library have also been initiated with a view to bringing information resources users and providers together, and staff there organise induction days for institutions.

- Other strong collections are held in the University of London libraries (most notably in Senate House, which now contains the collections of ILAS and ICwS, but also in University College London and King's

College London), Essex, Cambridge and Oxford (especially the Bodleian), the Cervantes Institute in London, the British Museum's Centre for Anthropology and The National Archives. All of this tends to confirm the general belief among LAC researchers that those working within the so-called 'golden triangle' have preferential access to resources, with adverse implications for other parts of the UK. Certainly, London is generally considered to be one of the best locations in the world for researching certain periods of Caribbean history.

- The University of Essex Collection of Latin American Art (ESCALA) comprises a distinguished collection of modern and contemporary art from the region, with particularly strong holdings from Brazil and Argentina, and an archive of related exhibition catalogues and printed ephemera. It is the only dedicated public collection of its kind in the UK and is among Europe's largest. As a resource for teaching and research, it is complemented by the university library's specialist holdings in the history of Latin American art.

- Additional, more specialist, collections that are worthy of note include those at the John Rylands Library (Manchester), the Caribbean Collection (Warwick) and the small Cuba-specialist Hennessy Collection (Nottingham).

- Librarians from many of these collections are organised in the Advisory Council of Latin American and Iberian Information Resources (ACLAIIR), which meets several times a year to exchange information on acquisitions and developments within the region as well as within UK higher education.[40] It forms part of the Red Europea de Información y Documentación sobre América Latina (REDIAL), a European association of libraries and documentation centres with collections on the region.[41] In 2002 ACLAIIR oversaw the production of the third edition of *Latin American and Caribbean Resources in the British Isles: a Directory* by ILAS. It provides details of national resources, including named special collections, specialist material, photographs and audio-visual materials.[42] The *Directory* is currently housed on the Latin American and Caribbean Research Portal on the ILAS website.[43]

40 See: http://aclaiir.org.uk/ (accessed 2 May 2013).

41 See: www.red-redial.net/redial.html (accessed 2 May 2013).

42 Alan Biggins and Valerie Cooper (2002) *Latin American and Caribbean Resources in the British Isles: a Directory* (London: Institute of Latin American Studies).

43 Available at: http://ilas.sas.ac.uk/portal.

Electronic sources and digitisation of some archival collections (including some in Spanish and some from Brazilian sources) have greatly facilitated access to some sources. Nonetheless, with few sources in LAC digitised, travel to the region to consult collections continues to be crucial.

Challenges faced by the Latin American and Caribbean research community

Despite the expansion and strength of the research being undertaken, and of the research community represented, scholars consider that the potential of UK-based researchers is constrained by several challenges, which are similar in some respects to those faced by other area studies scholars:

- Limitations on funding for research and graduate studentships.
- The lack of visibility of research on LAC, beyond the RAE 2008 sub-panel 47 on American Studies and Anglophone Area Studies and sub-panel 55 on Iberian and Latin American Languages, within current research environments that are structured to meet the criteria and assessment procedures associated with RAEs.

Trends in funding for LAC research

Researchers are only able to improve the range, scale and quality of their research if they are able to visit the relevant countries of the region to collect data, undertake fieldwork, meet counterparts and participate in academic activities. This all involves travel costs and may require leave of absence from researchers' institutions.

Research council funding

Especially relevant to this report are the ESRC and the AHRC, although differences in the type and presentation of data made publicly available through their websites makes true comparisons difficult, meaning that data for the two funding councils are not commensurate. In addition, the websites of both organisations are dynamic.

As far as financial support for postgraduates is concerned, there are in general very limited UK funding opportunities for masters and doctoral research, and no equivalents of the teaching and research assistantships offered by US universities.

Nonetheless, given the above caveats, the following characteristics emerge regarding absolute and relative levels of funding:

Economic and Social Research Council (ESRC)

The total amounts of funding for LAC research reached a record level of almost £1million in 2007. Despite the prevalent perception amongst researchers that funding levels from Research Councils UK (RCUK) for research on the region have diminished, analysis of the ESRC's responsive mode schemes between 2000–09 suggests that the number of awards and annual funding levels relating to the area has increased progressively for substantial grants and small awards (applications under £100,000 full economic costing (FEC)), postdoctoral fellowships and early career fellowships. It should be remembered, however, that the introduction of FEC in 2006 has had a considerable impact on the overall level of grant for some schemes, without necessarily reflecting a significant increase in the level of financial support available for research. Nevertheless, the number of awards has also increased from 24 in 2000–04 to 45 in 2005–09. While there were some substantial awards from 2005–09, only 11 were over £100,000 and half between £50,000 and £100,000. The small grant scheme closed in 2011.

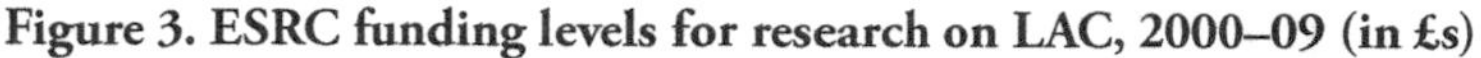

Figure 3. ESRC funding levels for research on LAC, 2000–09 (in £s)

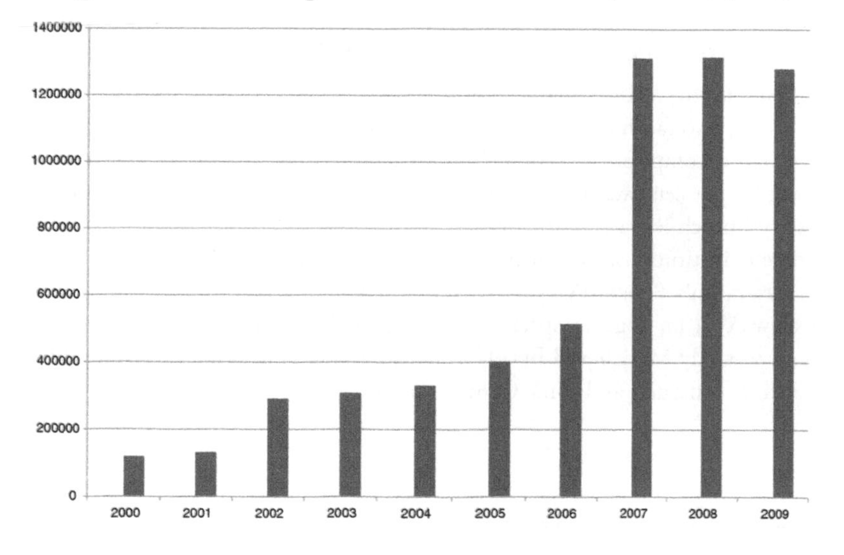

Source: Compiled from ESRC statistics from: www.esrc.ac.uk/impacts-and-findings/research-catalogue/index.aspx (accessed 10 Feb. 2011).[44]

44 The figures were compiled through a keyword search by individual country and region within LAC. The funds awarded include standard grants, postdoctoral awards and fellowships.

The total ESRC funding for LAC research over the decade in question was £5,997,045 awarded to academics within 36 different institutions. The 69 awards went to a wide range of institutions with none receiving more than five awards. Five universities received four or five awards (The Institute of Fiscal Studies, Bristol, Manchester, Oxford and Sheffield) and together their awards amounted to £2,201,523 or 36.7 per cent of the total funding.

In terms of ESRC doctoral studentships, prior to 2005 the number awarded for research on the LAC region generally reflected the amount of awards available. From 2011 studentships were allocated through 21 Doctoral Training Centres (DTCs) each organised by a consortium of universities. These have differing numbers of pathways. Two DTCs have a Language Based Area Studies (LBAS) pathway, but a prospective PhD can apply to work on LAC through other pathways. Data on postgraduate awards are monitored centrally but statistics are not available on how many are awarded specifically for LAC studies so it is not known whether the awards continue to reflect the general success rate. Initially, support for fieldwork was not included in the award, but this is now allocated to DTCs, although not specifically to the individual concerned.[45]

Arts and Humanities Research Council (AHRC)

In 2000–09 the AHRC awarded approximately £3,455,000 to academics in 27 institutions to facilitate research relating to Latin America (including research that had a comparative component to include other regions). Of this total, about 20 per cent was awarded for research leave. Research on the Caribbean received much less: approximately £210,500 was awarded to 11 academics in different institutions, of which nearly 65 per cent was awarded for research leave, and only £66,000 was awarded as a Research Grant (Standard).[46] Figure 4 shows that for country-specific research, the largest number of grants were made to study Mexico and Brazil, while no grants were made for the study of Ecuador, Venezuela and some Central American countries.

45 www.esrc.ac.uk/funding-and-guidance/postgraduates/dtc/index.aspx (accessed 21 Aug. 2014).

46 This is based on information from the AHRC database: www.ahrc.ac.uk/FundedResearch/Pages/ResearchStatistics.aspx (accessed 10 Oct. 2010). It should be noted that these data are very approximate, derived by carrying out a word search in the AHRC database of research titles for 'Latin America', the 'Caribbean', and for each individual country within the region; hence, the findings fail to identify any research grants for work on LAC-related topics whose title does not include any of these geographical key words. The funding totals include the postdoctoral categories of research leave, small grants, research grants (standard and speculative), resource enhancements, and research networks and workshops.

Figure 4. AHRC funding levels for research on LAC, 2000–09 (in £s)[47]

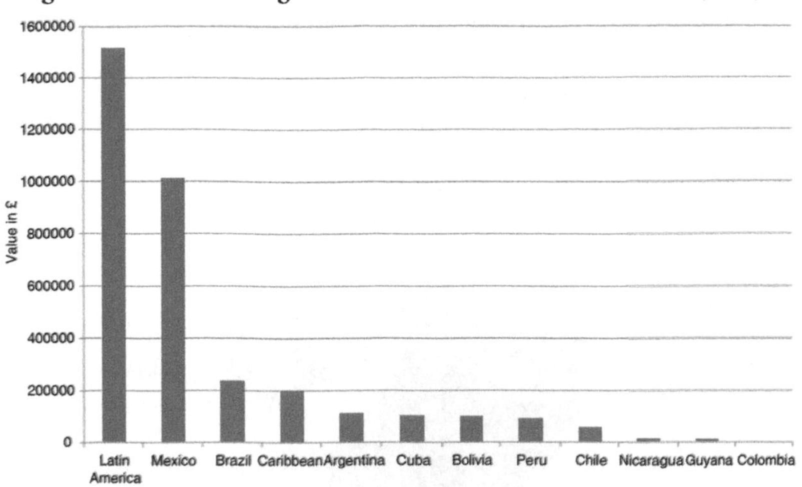

Source: AHRC database at: www.ahrc.ac.uk/FundedResearch/Pages/ResearchStatistics.aspx (accessed 10 Oct. 2010).

Despite the limited total funds awarded, LAC research appears to compare well with that of other regions, although, since research council databases do not categorise awards by geographical regions, this is not easy to verify. The findings in Figure 5, which refer only to modern languages and cultures, and only to the Research Grants (Standard) scheme, indicate that research on Latin America received the third largest amount out of a total of £22.5 million from the AHRC for the 2000–09 period, behind research funding for Celtic and French languages and culture, but slightly more than the amount awarded to research on the Middle East and Africa.

Until 2008, the AHRC's subject panels awarded studentships through its doctoral competition (including, more recently, its collaborative doctoral competitions), the Research Preparation Masters scheme and the Professional Preparation Masters scheme. Studentships for area studies are categorised according to the language and cultural groupings indicated in Figure 6. The total number of studentships awarded in area studies varies between the years, constituting between 9 per cent and 15 per cent of the total annual AHRC funding for all subjects. The precise numbers awarded between the language and cultural areas also vary marginally.

47 See note 46.

Figure 5. Comparative levels of AHRC Research Grants (Standard) awarded for modern languages and culture, 2000–09[48] (in £s)

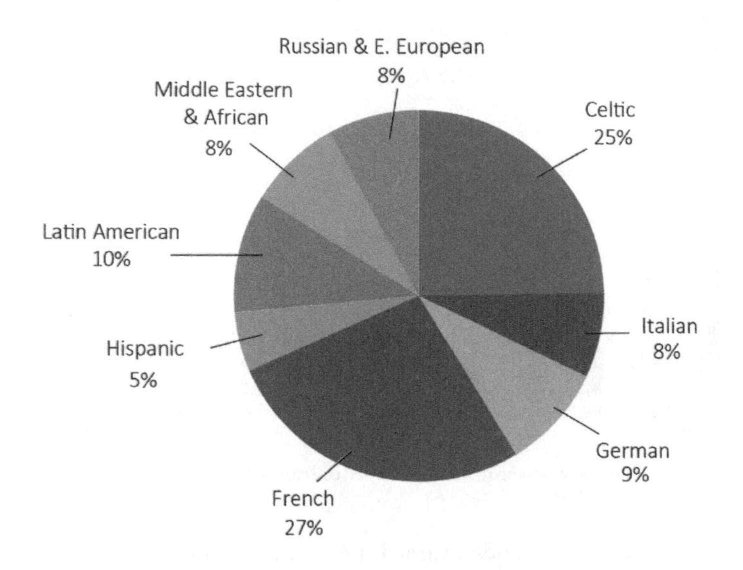

Source: Based on information taken from AHRC database at: www.ahrc.ac.uk/FundedResearch/BrowseResearch.aspx) (accessed Oct. 2010).

Between 2003–08, a total of 112 studentships were awarded under the combined category of Iberian and Latin American studies, of which 78 were for Latin American studies. The latter figure included 20 awards for masters courses. As shown in Figure 6, during that period AHRC support for studies and research on the region fell broadly within the range of other area studies subjects. Since 2009, doctoral studentships have been allocated under the Block Grant Partnerships (BGP) programme and only summary data is available by language and cultural area. These awards are allocated to institutions for five years. In all cases, the number of doctorates has declined, but of all the language and culture groups, the decline is greatest for Iberian and Latin American studies (about 20 per cent).

Of the 58 AHRC studentships awarded for doctoral research on LAC between 2003–08 (Figure 7), the highest number (8) were for research on Cuba, bringing it above Mexico and Brazil (and equal to the studentships awarded for research on the entire non-Hispanic Caribbean).

48 This diagram shows *only* those funds which were awarded within the category of Research Grants (Standard) within modern language areas, where it was indicated as a primary or combined subject. The figure excludes research on the Anglophone Caribbean, but 'French' includes the Francophone Caribbean.

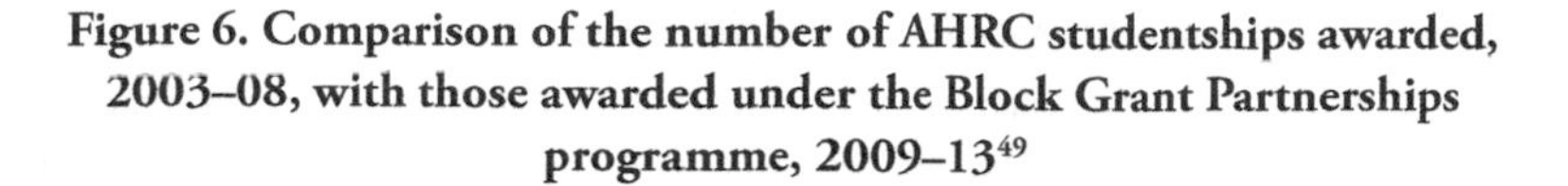

Figure 6. Comparison of the number of AHRC studentships awarded, 2003–08, with those awarded under the Block Grant Partnerships programme, 2009–13[49]

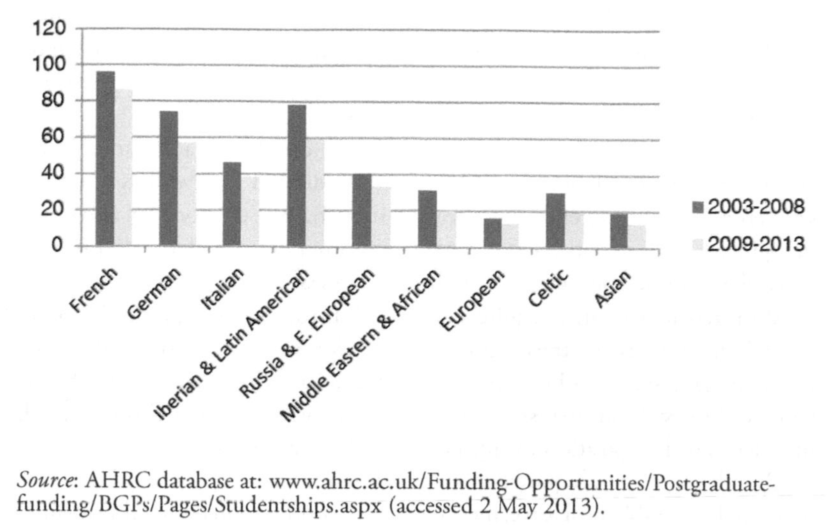

Source: AHRC database at: www.ahrc.ac.uk/Funding-Opportunities/Postgraduate-funding/BGPs/Pages/Studentships.aspx (accessed 2 May 2013).

Figure 7. Number of AHRC studentships awarded for doctoral research on LAC, 2003–08

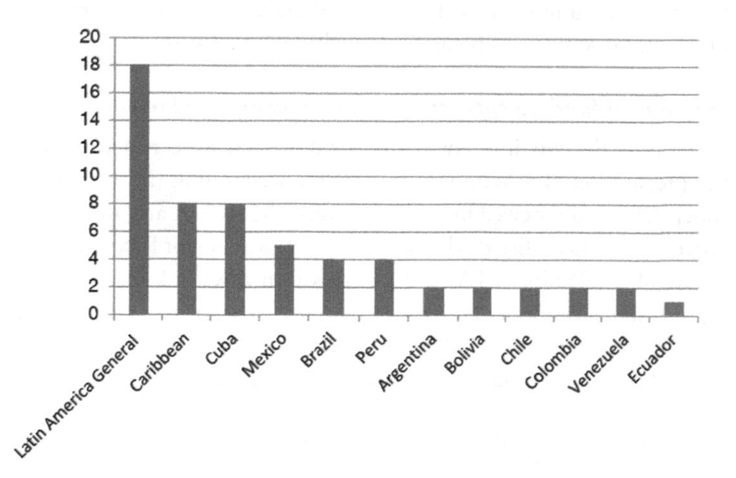

Source: AHRC database at: www.ahrc.ac.uk/FundedResearch/Pages/ResearchStatistics.aspx (accessed 10 Oct. 2010).

49 These figures do not disaggregate Latin American or Caribbean components of relevant language and culture groupings.

General comments on research council funding

Success rates for responsive mode standard research grants applications to AHRC and ESRC are low. These rates were 35 per cent and 27 per cent respectively in 2012–13.[50] Interviews indicated that many academics now clearly believe that access to research council funding for research on the region is more difficult, with some suggesting that success rates improve for research with comparative or UK-relevant components.

The trend within research councils is now clearly towards large grants and international collaboration.[51] Interviews indicated that while some LAC scholars welcome this trend, as supporting imaginative collaboration and cross-disciplinary projects, others fear that it may prejudice smaller-scale projects, especially in those undertaken by early career researchers.

Most researchers still require small and medium-sized grants in order to undertake necessary travel to the region (for sustained periods of several months). This seems to be of particular significance for early career scholars who need to establish themselves through fieldwork-based or archival research in order to be in a position to engage in collaborative work.

The advent of FEC requirements for universities has already raised the costs of research and sabbatical leave, fuelling greater competition between academics and institutions for limited funding and, in some cases, leading to fewer awards being available. Interview evidence suggested that some universities do not honour the commitment to support the 100 per cent buy-out of academics' time to enable the intended work to be undertaken, even when grants have been obtained, in some cases because of teaching requirements.

Research council funding opportunities for international research

There are currently two initiatives for Brazil, which have run concurrently with the preparation of a Memorandum of Understanding (MoU), signed in September 2009 and renewed in 2012, between the RCUK and the Fundação de Amparo à Pesquisa do Estado de São Paulo (Foundation for Research Support of the State of São Paulo, or FAPESP).[52] This formalises links to facilitate the funding of responsive-mode research, joint research seminars and preparation for partnerships to facilitate scholarly exchanges. This means that collaborative UK proposals will be peer-reviewed without the double jeopardy of individual

50 See www.ahrc.ac.uk/Funded-Research/Statistics/Pages/Competition-statistics.aspx (accessed 14 July 2014) and www.esrc.ac.uk/_images/ESRC_2012_13_Vital_Statistics_tcm8-29040.pdf (accessed 14 May 2013).

51 See AHRC Strategy 2013–18, available at: www.ahrc.ac.uk/News-and-Events/News/Documents/AHRC-Strategy-2013-18.pdf (accessed 14 July 2014).

52 www.rcuk.ac.uk/international/funding/collaboration/RCUKFAPESPmou/ (accessed 21 Aug. 2014).

national assessment by both funding authorities. Each funding partner of the collaboration would give financial support to their own respective researchers.

Other sources of funding

a) British Academy

The British Academy is important in facilitating overseas research and exchange activities, through a range of programmes, including its International Partnership and Mobility (IPM) and Small Research Grants schemes. Respondents recognise its crucial role in providing responsive mode funding earmarked for research, travel and international collaboration. The IPM initiative is the broad successor to such programmes as the UK-Latin American/Caribbean Link scheme. It supports the development of research partnerships between the UK and other areas of the world where research excellence would be strengthened by new, innovative initiatives and links, and explicitly includes partnerships between the UK and researchers in LAC as one of the priority regions.[53] The Small Research Grants scheme provides small-scale support to primary research more generally but includes overseas research, such as fieldwork and visits to archives. The Academy also participates with the Royal Society in the Newton International Fellowship scheme which brings postdoctoral scholars from anywhere in the world to the UK.[54]

Between 2006–12, under the IPM initiative and its predecessor the UK-LAC Link scheme, the Academy awarded approximately £660,000 (36 awards) to academics in 26 UK institutions to partner with researchers in the LAC region. Of these, four awards (approximately £74,000) were for partnerships with the Caribbean. Those remaining were for partnerships with 11 different Latin American countries. In 2012, 21 per cent of awards made under the IPM scheme were related to the LAC region (out of five regions covered) with a 25 per cent success rate for LAC applications.

British Academy funding for research on the LAC region, distributed through the Small Research Grants scheme, is shown in the data appearing in Table 5 below. It corresponds to funding allocations across nine geographical areas of the globe, between 2009–12, awarded on the basis of the quality of research proposed with no geographical quotas or restrictions. Fewer applications were submitted for LAC- related research compared to the majority of other regions. The success rate for LAC (26.6 per cent) was marginally lower when compared to other regions and the overall scheme average (28.8 per cent) over the period.

53 www.britac.ac.uk/funding/guide/intl/International_Partnership_and_Mobility.cfm (accessed 21 Aug. 2014).

54 www.britac.ac.uk/funding/guide/intl/newton_international_fellowships.cfm (accessed 21 Aug. 2014).

b) The Leverhulme Trust

The Trust was established in 1925 to support 'scholarships for the purposes of research and education.' Since that time, it has provided funding for research projects, fellowships, studentships, bursaries and prizes. The Trust operates across all the academic disciplines, the ambition being to support talented individuals in their research and professional training. Although it disburses about £60 million a year, the number of awards made to LAC research remains small. Between 2009–11 it made eight awards totalling £984,000 under its Research Project, International Network and Major Research Fellowship schemes.[55]

Table 5. British Academy applications and awards for small grants by region, 2009–12

Region	Applications	Awards	Per cent success	Value in £	Per cent of value
Asia	357	98	27.5	621,747	7.5
Australasia	13	3	23.1	22,122	0.3
Europe, including the UK	2,216	635	28.7	3,743,715	44.9
Russia/Eastern Europe	82	24	29.3	143,906	1.7
US/Canada	96	29	30.2	162,834	1.9
Middle East and Northern Africa	180	62	34.4	357,303	4.3
Sub-Saharan Africa	242	91	37.6	559,206	6.7
Latin America and the Caribbean	94	25	26.6	140,668	1.7
Unspecified	1,528	420	27.5	2,588,382	31.0
	4,808	**1,387**	***Av.* 28.8**	**8,339,883**	**100.0**

Av. = average

Source: British Academy database at: www.britac.ac.uk/funding/awards/index.cfm (accessed 3 May 2013).

55 See www.leverhulme.ac.uk/news/archive/grants.cfm (accessed 3 May 2013).

c) Banco Santander

Since 2007, Banco Santander has become an important funding source for UK-based research on Latin America, reflecting its own recognition of the commercial value of improved engagement with the region. It has signed collaborative agreements with 67 British universities, with the aim of establishing and strengthening international research networks.[56]

Banco Santander provides scholarships to study at UK universities to undergraduates and postgraduates from Argentina, Brazil, Chile, Colombia, Mexico, Peru, Portugal, Puerto Rico, Spain and Uruguay. Since 2007 it has disbursed over £500 million in the shape of scholarships, travel grants, support to special projects, academic and non-academic awards. Awards vary from university to university providing a highly valued mechanism by which departments can motivate and reward outstanding students and attract strong research candidates (including those from overseas) to their programmes.

d) Conference and other funds

Overseas conference attendance is an important research activity which seems unlikely to be diminished by greater ease of internet communication, since conferences allow researchers to exchange ideas, develop trust in formal and informal spaces, and develop collaborative initiatives.

Many universities offer small grants, but they are insufficient for fieldwork or more extensive visits for extensive data collection purposes. The lack of other region-specific funding sources (usually for relatively small amounts) is a genuine problem, preventing the development of established and newer researchers.

Impact of research assessment exercises

Changes occurring in higher education have effectively reduced the collective visibility of LAC scholarship within departments, universities and nationally. Despite HEFCE's explicit commitment to interdisciplinary work,[57] the structure of RAEs has reinforced disciplinary emphasis.

The 2008 RAE sub-panel for American Studies and Anglophone Area Studies considered only two submissions of Latin American or Caribbean scholars from Liverpool and London Metropolitan universities. As the Main Panel L's report recorded, many scholars were not submitted to area studies

56 See www.santander.co.uk/uk/santander-universities/about-us/our-partner-universities/ (accessed 15 Feb. 2013).

57 See, e.g., AHRC guidance at: www.ahrc.ac.uk/Funding-Opportunities/Research-funding/Pages/Research-funding.aspx, ESRC guidance at: www.esrc.ac.uk/funding-and-guidance/applicants/index.aspx, and REF 2014 Panel Criteria and Working Methods (January 2012), available at: www.ref.ac.uk/pubs/2012-01/.

panels, but to disciplinary panels, such as history, geography, politics, and social anthropology.[58] What this confirms is the difficulty of easily and properly assessing the strength of the research in LAC studies across the UK, as noted earlier.

In the forthcoming Research Excellence Framework (REF 2014), scholars of LAC studies can submit their applications to a choice of sub-panels. These include area studies (unit of assessment – UOA 27), which includes all areas of the world and lists LAC studies as one subject, and modern languages (UOA 28), which covers research on the languages, literatures, cultures and societies of all regions, including Latin America.[59] However, many academics and subject associations fear that HEFCE's fusion of the separate 2008 RAE panels into one overarching panel for all modern languages may further dilute the evaluation and importance of the area studies research on LAC that such departments carry out. A practical issue may be that there is a lack of expertise available for the panel to assess submissions effectively, although arrangements to bring in additional advisers have been and continue to be made. Another issue is the need in the REF 2014 to demonstrate impact. While this has been defined to include impact beyond the UK, and a wide range of possible indicators exist, there is nervousness about how this will be interpreted given it is the first time such an assessment is being made. This is, of course, not only an issue relating to LAC studies.

One consequence of the structure of RAEs is that LAC researchers often work within discipline boundaries and, specifically, to submit their research output to discipline-specific journals, even though it might be marginal to the central interest of the journal and not easily accessible to an interdisciplinary audience. Since a wide-ranging approach has been essential to research on LAC from the outset, this bodes ill for the subject, and at the same time fails to respond to the emphasis, stressed by government and funding bodies, on the importance of interdisciplinary research.

Constraints on dissemination and publication

Publication of research findings is a critical element of research activity, demonstrating the results of projects and the researcher's competence, and disseminating conclusions to others. In many respects, the field open to researchers in LAC studies is greater than it has ever been, with a plethora of publishing outlets.

58 RAE 2008 subject overview reports are available at: www.rae.ac.uk/pubs/2009/ov/ (accessed 10 Jan. 2014).

59 REF2014 Units of Assessment are available at: www.ref.ac.uk/panels/unitsofassessment/ (accessed 15 Feb. 2013).

In the UK alone there are the multidisciplinary *Bulletin of Latin American Research* and *Journal of Latin American Studies*, the *Journal of Latin American Cultural Studies* (as well as two broader culture-oriented journals for Iberian and Latin American research, the *Bulletin of Spanish Studies* and *Bulletin of Hispanic Studies*), and discipline-specialist journals such as *Journal of Latin American and Caribbean Anthropology* and the newer *Latin American and Caribbean Ethnic Studies*. The *Journal of Latin American Studies* has the highest impact factor in the world of all journals in the field.[60]

There are also series of books produced by notable publishers. Among these the following stand out: the ILAS in-house series and the 'Studies of the Americas' series with Palgrave, edited by UCL Institute for the Americas, both of which include Caribbean as well as Latin American titles on a range of disciplines, Frank Cass and Macmillan Caribbean. Wada Bagi, Ian Randal and University of the West Indies also provide additional outlets for Caribbeanists and the appearance of the latter two has revitalised Caribbean book offerings.

However, this report believes that the publishing strategies of many academics have been affected over the last ten years by the RAE, journal rankings, citation indices, research league tables and so on. Academics have been encouraged or pressured by their institutions to publish articles in discipline-specific journals rather than interdisciplinary journals, and to publish in English (not in foreign languages). The interviews undertaken for this report suggested that early career researchers have felt this more acutely.

Nearly all scholars working on the non-English speaking world consider it important to publish in other languages as a means of disseminating research findings and of engaging with scholars from the region. Many of those surveyed during the research for this report publish in either Spanish or Portuguese, as a matter of academic responsibility, and many young scholars aspire to do so in the near future. Several also appreciate the importance in terms of the responsibility of providing research feedback to national and local communities. In principle, any research evaluation criteria which recognise the importance of knowledge transfer and exchange, community outreach and dissemination could be met by publication in non-English language outlets.

Other activities, including reference works (such as encyclopaedia entries), popular literature (such as travel explorations), text books and book reviews, are valued by researchers as interesting components of their scholarly work, as well as an expression of their freedom to define their own publishing activities.

At the time of writing, the UK Government funding councils and the RCUK are committed to an open access policy, which may have a significant impact on scholars' publishing strategies. Concerns have been expressed about

60 See Web of Knowledge, available at: http://admin-apps.webofknowledge.com/JCR/JCR (accessed 22 Sep. 2013).

its potential impact where resources are less readily available to pay the article processing charges (APCs) that journals will require. This may, however, be mitigated by the proposed green model, which insists on an embargo period but does not require an APC. In the UK the proposal to link the policy to the REF may discourage scholars from publishing in international journals that are not compliant with this policy. There are also fears that it may have an adverse impact on the income of learned societies, such as the SLAS, whose journal proceeds currently fund a range of academic activities in their fields.[61]

Reflections

Although the research for this report encountered some methodological problems (arising from the dispersion of scholars beyond LAC-specialising departments or schools, the failure of social science researchers, in particular, to identify themselves as LAC scholars and the difficulty of identifying many LAC-focused projects in funding bodies' records), the editors are confident that the overall picture presented is accurate in terms of the general trends and the majority of LAC-focused research in the UK.

The most obvious conclusion is that the strategy outlined by the 1965 Parry Report seems to have borne fruit over the decades in the growth and spread of research, expertise and teaching in Latin American studies, which now extends well beyond the original 'Parry centres'. Certainly, aspects of Latin America are now studied (including at undergraduate level) in a vastly increased range of departments, centres and institutions than was the case in the 1960s. This, in turn, has either generated or been reflected in an increase in postgraduate and postdoctoral research on the region. One dimension of this expansion has been a broadening of the disciplines involved in Latin American studies research, with the growth in cultural studies being especially strong.

All of this has strengthened overall LAC expertise in terms of individuals and institutions at a time when increased UK interest (most obviously in government and business) in the region is likely to create greater opportunities for academics and departments specialising in the region.

Behind (and despite) this overall positive picture, however, the report has unearthed some areas of concern within LAC research and knowledge in the UK's higher education sector:

61 Rebecca Darley, Daniel Reynolds and Chris Wickham (2014) *Open Access Journals in Humanities and Social Science* (London: The British Academy), available at: www.britac.ac.uk/openaccess/index.cfm (accessed 30 Jan. 2014); for further reading see Chris Wickham and Nigel Vincent (eds.) (2013) *Debating Open Access* (London: British Academy), available at: www.britac.ac.uk/openaccess/debatingopenaccess.cfm (accessed 30 Jan. 2014).

- While it might be argued that the spread of Latin American studies beyond the 'Parry centres' made these institutions somewhat redundant historically, it remains a source of disquiet that two of these centres (Liverpool and Glasgow) have either closed or become totally absorbed by another school, losing their separate identity for funding and expertise. Equally, the closure of one of the UK's two Caribbeanist centres, at LMU, must be a matter of serious concern for the UK's ability to sustain the study of the region. The centres play a vital role in sustaining postgraduate teaching programmes and in acting as foci for research activities in their wider regions and nationally. The scholarly landscape is more fragmented making collaboration and coordination between scholars in the field less easily achieved.

- The dispersion of LAC scholars beyond the traditional centres, often in discipline-based departments, makes the study of the region vulnerable in the face of retirements and changes in individual university policies. While the age structure of the academic profession as a whole means that many senior staff are approaching retirement age, the case is particularly acute in Latin American studies where many posts were created with Parry funding in the late 1960s and the 1970s. It is disturbing that a number of high-profile LAC posts are not currently being filled.

- Despite the recognition in the RAE 2008 and REF 2014 that interdisciplinary research, which encompasses area studies, should be assessed on an equal basis to disciplinary research, the way in which RAEs are structured has often worked against the growth or health of the discipline area. As the report has highlighted, there are other reasons behind this too. The regional expertise of scholars has often become of lesser consideration than the contribution their research can make to a specific discipline.

- The location of scholars of Latin America has shifted. History departments appear reluctant to appoint to Latin American-focused posts, which are increasingly located in language departments, while many academics in social science fields, especially politics and international relations, take a theoretical or comparative approach. Although there is clearly space for both, it does mean that an area studies approach to Latin American studies which combines knowledge of the local context, language learning and discipline training is in danger of being undermined such that it will be unable to address key and social, political and economic issues and developments that are currently of increasing international interest.

- Because scholars tend to be scattered across discipline-based departments, the field is vulnerable to changes in broader government or university policies. While the growth of Latin American cultural studies in language departments is to be welcomed, the experience of the post-1992 higher education sector, where many previously flourishing languages departments/schools have closed or been downgraded to be language training units, thereby undermining their commitment to LAC research in the humanities and social sciences, suggest that they may not have a secure future.

- While levels of research and postgraduate funding for LAC studies appear comparable to those for other regions, scholarly interest focuses on relatively few countries, namely Mexico, Brazil and Cuba, while some countries remain little studied, including most of Central America. The dearth of academic expertise on significant parts of Latin America must be a concern at a time when there is increasing interest in engaging with the region.

- While the overall level of funding may not have fallen, sources of financial support for small-scale projects and short field visits to the region have declined. This coincides with the research councils' emphasis on large-scale projects and, in the case of postgraduates, in the delegation of the distribution of fieldwork support to higher education institutions rather than to individual students.

- Funding for postgraduate students from LAC has increased in some countries such as Brazil, but its availability is highly dependent on political decisions in the region. Meanwhile, many in the sector fear that any increase in fee levels will make LAC research in the UK higher education sphere much less competitive than either the United States or the rest of the EU, despite its inherent strengths in terms of expertise.

CPSIA information can be obtained at www.ICGtesting.com
Printed in the USA
BVOW10s1346010215

385807BV00002B/5/P